50 Sweet and Savory Breakfast Recipes

By: Kelly Johnson

Table of Contents

- Classic Buttermilk Pancakes with Maple Syrup
- Blueberry Lemon Ricotta Pancakes
- Cinnamon French Toast with Whipped Cream
- Belgian Waffles with Fresh Berries
- Chocolate Chip Banana Bread Muffins
- Apple Cinnamon Oatmeal with Walnuts
- Strawberry Shortcake Crepes
- Honey & Greek Yogurt Parfait with Granola
- Carrot Cake Oatmeal with Cream Cheese Drizzle
- Peanut Butter & Banana Overnight Oats
- Pumpkin Spice Pancakes with Pecan Crunch
- Mocha Smoothie Bowl with Dark Chocolate
- Raspberry Almond Croissant Bake
- Maple Glazed Donuts
- Chia Seed Pudding with Mango & Coconut
- Sweet Potato & Cinnamon Oatmeal
- Baked Apple Crisp with Almond Butter
- Nutella & Strawberry Stuffed French Toast
- Lemon Poppy Seed Muffins
- Chocolate Hazelnut Crepes
- Cherry Almond Scones
- Vanilla Bean Greek Yogurt with Honey
- Mixed Berry & Chia Jam Toast
- Warm Pear & Cardamom Oatmeal
- Maple Walnut Granola with Yogurt
- Classic Eggs Benedict with Hollandaise Sauce
- Avocado Toast with Poached Egg & Sriracha
- Cheddar & Spinach Scrambled Eggs
- Sausage & Cheese Breakfast Biscuits
- Smoked Salmon & Cream Cheese Bagel
- Chorizo & Egg Breakfast Burrito
- Ham & Swiss Croissant Sandwich
- Bacon & Egg Breakfast Tacos
- Sweet Potato & Black Bean Breakfast Hash
- Spinach & Feta Omelet
- Breakfast Quesadilla with Salsa

- Savory Breakfast Galette with Mushrooms
- Biscuits & Country Sausage Gravy
- Baked Shakshuka with Feta
- Breakfast Fried Rice with Egg & Bacon
- Crispy Hash Browns with Parmesan
- Italian Breakfast Frittata with Sun-Dried Tomatoes
- Cottage Cheese & Smoked Salmon Bowl
- Cheesy Grits with Butter & Poached Egg
- Avocado & Turkey Breakfast Wrap
- Roasted Veggie & Egg Breakfast Bowl
- Greek Yogurt & Savory Granola Bowl
- Breakfast Polenta with Garlic & Herbs
- Scrambled Eggs with Chorizo & Peppers
- Croque Madame with Gruyère & Ham

Classic Buttermilk Pancakes with Maple Syrup

Ingredients:

- 1 ½ cups all-purpose flour
- 2 tbsp sugar
- 1 tsp baking powder
- ½ tsp baking soda
- ½ tsp salt
- 1 ¼ cups buttermilk
- 1 egg
- 2 tbsp melted butter
- 1 tsp vanilla extract
- Maple syrup for serving

Instructions:

1. Whisk dry ingredients together.
2. In a separate bowl, mix buttermilk, egg, melted butter, and vanilla.
3. Combine wet and dry ingredients (do not overmix).
4. Cook on a greased skillet over medium heat until golden brown on both sides.
5. Serve with maple syrup.

Blueberry Lemon Ricotta Pancakes

Ingredients:

- 1 ½ cups all-purpose flour
- 1 tsp baking powder
- ½ tsp baking soda
- ¼ tsp salt
- ¼ cup sugar
- ¾ cup ricotta cheese
- ¾ cup milk
- 2 eggs
- 1 tbsp lemon zest
- ½ cup fresh blueberries

Instructions:

1. Mix dry ingredients.
2. In a separate bowl, mix ricotta, milk, eggs, and lemon zest.
3. Combine wet and dry ingredients, then fold in blueberries.
4. Cook on a skillet over medium heat until golden brown.

Cinnamon French Toast with Whipped Cream

Ingredients:

- 4 slices thick-cut bread
- 2 eggs
- ½ cup milk
- 1 tsp cinnamon
- 1 tsp vanilla extract
- 1 tbsp sugar
- 1 tbsp butter

Whipped Cream:

- ½ cup heavy cream
- 1 tbsp powdered sugar

Instructions:

1. Whisk eggs, milk, cinnamon, vanilla, and sugar.
2. Dip bread into the mixture, coating both sides.
3. Cook in a buttered skillet until golden brown.
4. Whip heavy cream and powdered sugar until soft peaks form.
5. Serve French toast with whipped cream.

Belgian Waffles with Fresh Berries

Ingredients:

- 2 cups all-purpose flour
- 1 tbsp sugar
- 1 tbsp baking powder
- ½ tsp salt
- 2 eggs, separated
- 1 ¾ cups milk
- ½ cup melted butter
- 1 tsp vanilla extract
- 1 cup mixed fresh berries

Instructions:

1. Whisk together dry ingredients.
2. In a separate bowl, mix egg yolks, milk, butter, and vanilla.
3. Beat egg whites until stiff peaks form and fold into batter.
4. Cook in a preheated waffle iron until golden brown.
5. Serve with fresh berries.

Chocolate Chip Banana Bread Muffins

Ingredients:

- 2 ripe bananas, mashed
- ½ cup sugar
- ¼ cup melted butter
- 1 egg
- 1 tsp vanilla extract
- 1 ½ cups all-purpose flour
- 1 tsp baking soda
- ½ tsp salt
- ½ cup chocolate chips

Instructions:

1. Preheat oven to **350°F (175°C)**.
2. Mix mashed bananas, sugar, melted butter, egg, and vanilla.
3. Stir in flour, baking soda, and salt.
4. Fold in chocolate chips.
5. Fill muffin tins and bake for **18-20 minutes**.

Apple Cinnamon Oatmeal with Walnuts

Ingredients:

- 1 cup rolled oats
- 2 cups milk or water
- ½ cup diced apples
- ½ tsp cinnamon
- 1 tbsp maple syrup
- 2 tbsp chopped walnuts

Instructions:

1. Cook oats in milk or water.
2. Stir in apples, cinnamon, and maple syrup.
3. Top with chopped walnuts before serving.

Strawberry Shortcake Crêpes

Ingredients:

- 1 cup all-purpose flour
- 1 ¼ cups milk
- 2 eggs
- 1 tbsp sugar
- 1 tsp vanilla extract
- 1 tbsp butter, melted

Filling:

- 1 cup sliced strawberries
- ½ cup whipped cream
- 1 tbsp honey

Instructions:

1. Blend crêpe batter and let rest for **10 minutes**.
2. Cook thin crêpes in a buttered pan.
3. Fill with whipped cream and strawberries, then drizzle with honey.

Honey & Greek Yogurt Parfait with Granola

Ingredients:

- 1 cup Greek yogurt
- ½ cup granola
- 1 tbsp honey
- ½ cup mixed berries

Instructions:

1. Layer yogurt and granola in a glass.
2. Drizzle with honey and top with berries.

Carrot Cake Oatmeal with Cream Cheese Drizzle

Ingredients:

- 1 cup rolled oats
- 2 cups milk or water
- ½ cup shredded carrots
- ½ tsp cinnamon
- 1 tbsp maple syrup
- 2 tbsp chopped walnuts

Cream Cheese Drizzle:

- 2 tbsp cream cheese
- 1 tbsp honey
- 1 tbsp milk

Instructions:

1. Cook oats in milk or water.
2. Stir in shredded carrots, cinnamon, and maple syrup.
3. Mix cream cheese drizzle and pour over oatmeal before serving.

Peanut Butter & Banana Overnight Oats

Ingredients:

- ½ cup rolled oats
- ½ cup almond milk
- 1 tbsp chia seeds
- 1 tbsp peanut butter
- ½ banana, sliced
- 1 tsp honey

Instructions:

1. Mix oats, almond milk, chia seeds, peanut butter, and honey in a jar.
2. Refrigerate overnight.
3. Stir before serving and top with banana slices.

Pumpkin Spice Pancakes with Pecan Crunch

Ingredients:

- 1 ½ cups all-purpose flour
- 1 tbsp sugar
- 1 tsp baking powder
- ½ tsp baking soda
- ½ tsp salt
- ½ tsp pumpkin spice
- ½ cup pumpkin purée
- 1 cup milk
- 1 egg
- 2 tbsp melted butter
- ½ cup chopped pecans

Instructions:

1. Mix dry ingredients in a bowl.
2. In another bowl, whisk pumpkin purée, milk, egg, and butter.
3. Combine wet and dry ingredients.
4. Cook pancakes on a greased skillet until golden.
5. Top with pecans and maple syrup.

Mocha Smoothie Bowl with Dark Chocolate

Ingredients:

- 1 frozen banana
- ½ cup cold brew coffee
- ½ cup almond milk
- 1 tbsp cocoa powder
- 1 tbsp almond butter
- 1 tbsp dark chocolate shavings

Instructions:

1. Blend banana, coffee, almond milk, cocoa powder, and almond butter until smooth.
2. Pour into a bowl and top with dark chocolate shavings.

Raspberry Almond Croissant Bake

Ingredients:

- 4 croissants, torn into pieces
- 1 cup raspberries
- 1 cup milk
- 3 eggs
- ¼ cup sugar
- 1 tsp vanilla extract
- ¼ cup sliced almonds

Instructions:

1. Preheat oven to **350°F (175°C)**.
2. Whisk milk, eggs, sugar, and vanilla.
3. Toss croissant pieces with raspberries and almonds.
4. Pour mixture over croissants and let soak for **10 minutes**.
5. Bake for **25 minutes** until golden.

Maple Glazed Donuts

Ingredients:

- 2 cups all-purpose flour
- 1 tsp baking powder
- ½ tsp salt
- ½ cup sugar
- ½ cup milk
- 2 tbsp melted butter
- 1 egg
- 1 tsp vanilla extract

Maple Glaze:

- ½ cup powdered sugar
- 2 tbsp maple syrup
- 1 tbsp milk

Instructions:

1. Preheat oven to **350°F (175°C)**.
2. Mix dry ingredients, then stir in wet ingredients.
3. Pipe batter into a greased donut pan and bake for **12-15 minutes**.
4. Whisk glaze ingredients and dip donuts when cooled.

Chia Seed Pudding with Mango & Coconut

Ingredients:

- ¼ cup chia seeds
- 1 cup coconut milk
- 1 tbsp honey
- ½ cup diced mango
- 2 tbsp shredded coconut

Instructions:

1. Mix chia seeds, coconut milk, and honey.
2. Refrigerate overnight.
3. Top with mango and shredded coconut before serving.

Sweet Potato & Cinnamon Oatmeal

Ingredients:

- 1 cup rolled oats
- 2 cups milk or water
- ½ cup mashed sweet potato
- ½ tsp cinnamon
- 1 tbsp maple syrup
- 2 tbsp chopped walnuts

Instructions:

1. Cook oats in milk or water.
2. Stir in mashed sweet potato, cinnamon, and maple syrup.
3. Top with walnuts before serving.

Baked Apple Crisp with Almond Butter

Ingredients:

- 2 apples, sliced
- 1 tbsp maple syrup
- ½ tsp cinnamon
- ½ cup rolled oats
- ¼ cup almond butter
- 2 tbsp chopped almonds

Instructions:

1. Preheat oven to **375°F (190°C)**.
2. Toss apples with maple syrup and cinnamon.
3. Mix oats, almond butter, and almonds, then sprinkle over apples.
4. Bake for **20 minutes** until golden.

Nutella & Strawberry Stuffed French Toast

Ingredients:

- 4 slices thick-cut bread
- 2 tbsp Nutella
- ½ cup sliced strawberries
- 2 eggs
- ½ cup milk
- 1 tsp vanilla extract
- 1 tbsp butter

Instructions:

1. Spread Nutella on two slices of bread, add strawberries, and top with remaining bread.
2. Whisk eggs, milk, and vanilla.
3. Dip sandwiches in the mixture and cook in butter until golden brown.

Lemon Poppy Seed Muffins

Ingredients:

- 2 cups all-purpose flour
- ½ cup sugar
- 1 tsp baking powder
- ½ tsp baking soda
- ½ tsp salt
- 1 tbsp poppy seeds
- ½ cup milk
- ¼ cup melted butter
- 1 egg
- 2 tbsp lemon juice
- 1 tsp lemon zest

Instructions:

1. Preheat oven to **375°F (190°C)**.
2. Mix dry ingredients, then stir in wet ingredients.
3. Fill muffin tins and bake for **18-20 minutes**.

Chocolate Hazelnut Crêpes

Ingredients:

- 1 cup all-purpose flour
- 1 ¼ cups milk
- 2 eggs
- 1 tbsp sugar
- 1 tsp vanilla extract
- 1 tbsp butter, melted

Filling:

- ¼ cup Nutella
- ¼ cup chopped hazelnuts

Instructions:

1. Blend crêpe batter and let rest for **10 minutes**.
2. Cook thin crêpes in a buttered pan.
3. Spread Nutella inside, sprinkle with hazelnuts, and fold.

Cherry Almond Scones

Ingredients:

- 2 cups all-purpose flour
- ¼ cup sugar
- 1 tbsp baking powder
- ½ tsp salt
- ½ cup cold butter, cubed
- ½ cup milk
- 1 egg
- ½ cup fresh or dried cherries
- ¼ cup sliced almonds

Instructions:

1. Preheat oven to **400°F (200°C)**.
2. Mix dry ingredients, then cut in butter until crumbly.
3. Stir in milk, egg, cherries, and almonds.
4. Shape dough into a circle, cut into wedges, and bake for **15-18 minutes**.

Vanilla Bean Greek Yogurt with Honey

Ingredients:

- 1 cup Greek yogurt
- 1/2 tsp vanilla bean paste or extract
- 1 tbsp honey
- 2 tbsp chopped walnuts (optional)

Instructions:

1. Mix Greek yogurt with vanilla bean paste.
2. Drizzle with honey and sprinkle with walnuts before serving.

Mixed Berry & Chia Jam Toast

Ingredients:

- 2 slices whole grain bread, toasted
- 1/2 cup mixed berries (strawberries, raspberries, blueberries)
- 1 tbsp chia seeds
- 1 tbsp honey or maple syrup

Instructions:

1. Heat berries and honey in a saucepan until soft.
2. Mash berries and stir in chia seeds. Let sit for **10 minutes** until thickened.
3. Spread chia jam on toast and serve.

Warm Pear & Cardamom Oatmeal

Ingredients:

- 1 cup rolled oats
- 2 cups milk or water
- 1/2 pear, diced
- 1/4 tsp cardamom
- 1 tbsp honey
- 1 tbsp chopped almonds

Instructions:

1. Cook oats in milk or water.
2. Stir in diced pear, cardamom, and honey.
3. Top with chopped almonds before serving.

Maple Walnut Granola with Yogurt

Ingredients:

- 2 cups rolled oats
- 1/2 cup chopped walnuts
- 1/4 cup maple syrup
- 1 tsp cinnamon
- 2 tbsp melted coconut oil

Instructions:

1. Preheat oven to **325°F (165°C)**.
2. Mix all ingredients and spread on a baking sheet.
3. Bake for **15-20 minutes**, stirring halfway.
4. Serve over Greek yogurt.

Classic Eggs Benedict with Hollandaise Sauce

Ingredients:

- 2 English muffins, toasted
- 4 slices Canadian bacon
- 4 poached eggs

Hollandaise Sauce:

- 3 egg yolks
- 1/2 cup melted butter
- 1 tbsp lemon juice
- Salt & cayenne pepper

Instructions:

1. Poach eggs in simmering water.
2. Cook Canadian bacon until browned.
3. Blend egg yolks, lemon juice, and melted butter for hollandaise sauce.
4. Assemble muffins with bacon, eggs, and hollandaise.

Avocado Toast with Poached Egg & Sriracha

Ingredients:

- 2 slices sourdough bread, toasted
- 1 ripe avocado, mashed
- 2 poached eggs
- 1/2 tsp red pepper flakes
- 1 tsp Sriracha
- Salt & black pepper

Instructions:

1. Spread mashed avocado on toast.
2. Top with poached eggs and drizzle with Sriracha.
3. Sprinkle with red pepper flakes, salt, and pepper.

Cheddar & Spinach Scrambled Eggs

Ingredients:

- 3 eggs
- 1/4 cup shredded cheddar cheese
- 1/2 cup fresh spinach, chopped
- 1 tbsp butter
- Salt & black pepper

Instructions:

1. Sauté spinach in butter until wilted.
2. Whisk eggs, then cook over low heat.
3. Stir in cheddar cheese and spinach before serving.

Sausage & Cheese Breakfast Biscuits

Ingredients:

- 2 cups all-purpose flour
- 1 tbsp baking powder
- 1/2 tsp salt
- 1/2 cup cold butter, cubed
- 1/2 cup cooked crumbled sausage
- 1/2 cup shredded cheddar cheese
- 3/4 cup milk

Instructions:

1. Preheat oven to **400°F (200°C)**.
2. Mix dry ingredients, then cut in butter until crumbly.
3. Stir in sausage, cheese, and milk until combined.
4. Drop spoonfuls onto a baking sheet and bake for **12-15 minutes**.

Smoked Salmon & Cream Cheese Bagel

Ingredients:

- 2 bagels, halved and toasted
- 4 tbsp cream cheese
- 4 oz smoked salmon
- 1 tbsp capers
- 1/4 small red onion, thinly sliced

Instructions:

1. Spread cream cheese on toasted bagels.
2. Top with smoked salmon, capers, and red onion.

Chorizo & Egg Breakfast Burrito

Ingredients:

- 2 large eggs
- 1/2 cup cooked chorizo
- 1 flour tortilla
- 1/4 cup shredded cheese
- 1 tbsp salsa

Instructions:

1. Scramble eggs with cooked chorizo.
2. Fill tortilla with eggs, chorizo, cheese, and salsa.
3. Wrap and serve.

Ham & Swiss Croissant Sandwich

Ingredients:

- 2 croissants, halved
- 4 slices ham
- 2 slices Swiss cheese
- 2 tbsp Dijon mustard
- 1 tbsp butter

Instructions:

1. Preheat oven to **375°F (190°C)**.
2. Spread Dijon mustard inside croissants.
3. Layer ham and Swiss cheese, then close sandwiches.
4. Brush with butter and bake for **5-7 minutes** until golden and melty.

Bacon & Egg Breakfast Tacos

Ingredients:

- 2 large eggs, scrambled
- 4 small flour or corn tortillas
- 4 slices bacon, cooked and crumbled
- 1/4 cup shredded cheddar cheese
- 1 tbsp chopped cilantro
- 1 tbsp salsa

Instructions:

1. Warm tortillas.
2. Fill with scrambled eggs, bacon, and cheese.
3. Top with cilantro and salsa before serving.

Sweet Potato & Black Bean Breakfast Hash

Ingredients:

- 1 sweet potato, diced
- 1/2 cup black beans, drained and rinsed
- 1/2 tsp cumin
- 1/2 tsp smoked paprika
- 1 tbsp olive oil
- 2 fried eggs (optional)

Instructions:

1. Sauté sweet potatoes in olive oil over medium heat until tender.
2. Stir in black beans, cumin, and smoked paprika.
3. Serve with fried eggs if desired.

Spinach & Feta Omelet

Ingredients:

- 3 eggs
- 1/2 cup fresh spinach, chopped
- 1/4 cup crumbled feta cheese
- 1 tbsp butter
- Salt & black pepper

Instructions:

1. Whisk eggs with salt and pepper.
2. Sauté spinach in butter until wilted.
3. Pour in eggs and cook until set.
4. Sprinkle with feta, fold, and serve.

Breakfast Quesadilla with Salsa

Ingredients:

- 2 flour tortillas
- 2 eggs, scrambled
- 1/2 cup shredded cheese
- 1/4 cup cooked bacon or sausage
- 2 tbsp salsa

Instructions:

1. Heat a skillet and place one tortilla down.
2. Sprinkle with cheese, scrambled eggs, and meat.
3. Place the second tortilla on top and cook until golden brown on both sides.
4. Slice and serve with salsa.

Savory Breakfast Galette with Mushrooms

Ingredients:

- 1 sheet puff pastry
- 1/2 cup sautéed mushrooms
- 1/4 cup crumbled goat cheese
- 1 egg yolk (for brushing)
- 1 tsp fresh thyme

Instructions:

1. Preheat oven to **375°F (190°C)**.
2. Roll out pastry and spread mushrooms and goat cheese in the center.
3. Fold edges, brush with egg yolk, and bake for **20-25 minutes**.
4. Sprinkle with thyme before serving.

Biscuits & Country Sausage Gravy

Ingredients:

- 2 cups all-purpose flour
- 1 tbsp baking powder
- 1/2 tsp salt
- 1/2 cup cold butter, cubed
- 3/4 cup milk

Sausage Gravy:

- 1/2 lb breakfast sausage
- 2 tbsp butter
- 2 tbsp flour
- 1 1/2 cups milk
- Salt & black pepper

Instructions:

1. Preheat oven to **400°F (200°C)**.
2. Mix dry ingredients, cut in butter, and stir in milk. Form dough and bake biscuits for **12-15 minutes**.
3. Cook sausage in a pan, then add butter and flour. Slowly whisk in milk to make gravy.
4. Serve biscuits with sausage gravy.

Baked Shakshuka with Feta

Ingredients:

- 1 tbsp olive oil
- 1/2 onion, chopped
- 1 bell pepper, sliced
- 2 cloves garlic, minced
- 1 tsp cumin
- 1 tsp smoked paprika
- 1 can (14 oz) crushed tomatoes
- 4 eggs
- 1/4 cup crumbled feta cheese
- Fresh parsley, for garnish

Instructions:

1. Preheat oven to **375°F (190°C)**.
2. Sauté onion and bell pepper in olive oil until softened.
3. Add garlic, cumin, paprika, and crushed tomatoes. Simmer for **10 minutes**.
4. Make wells in the sauce and crack eggs into them.
5. Bake for **10-12 minutes**, then top with feta and parsley.

Breakfast Fried Rice with Egg & Bacon

Ingredients:

- 1 cup cooked rice (preferably day-old)
- 2 slices bacon, chopped
- 1/2 cup diced bell peppers
- 1/2 cup peas
- 2 eggs, scrambled
- 1 tbsp soy sauce
- 1 tsp sesame oil

Instructions:

1. Cook bacon until crispy. Remove and set aside.
2. Sauté bell peppers and peas in bacon grease.
3. Add rice, soy sauce, and sesame oil, then mix in scrambled eggs.
4. Stir in crispy bacon before serving.

Crispy Hash Browns with Parmesan

Ingredients:

- 2 russet potatoes, grated
- 2 tbsp butter
- 1/4 cup grated Parmesan cheese
- 1/2 tsp garlic powder
- Salt & black pepper

Instructions:

1. Squeeze out excess moisture from grated potatoes.
2. Heat butter in a skillet and press potatoes into an even layer.
3. Cook until crispy on both sides.
4. Sprinkle with Parmesan and season before serving.

Italian Breakfast Frittata with Sun-Dried Tomatoes

Ingredients:

- 6 eggs
- 1/4 cup milk
- 1/2 cup sun-dried tomatoes, chopped
- 1/2 cup spinach, chopped
- 1/2 cup shredded mozzarella or Parmesan cheese
- 1 tbsp olive oil
- Salt & black pepper

Instructions:

1. Preheat oven to **375°F (190°C)**.
2. Whisk eggs, milk, salt, and pepper.
3. Heat olive oil in an oven-safe skillet and sauté spinach and sun-dried tomatoes.
4. Pour in the egg mixture and sprinkle with cheese.
5. Cook on the stovetop for **2 minutes**, then transfer to the oven and bake for **12-15 minutes** until set.

Cottage Cheese & Smoked Salmon Bowl

Ingredients:

- 1 cup cottage cheese
- 2 oz smoked salmon
- 1 tbsp capers
- 1/4 small red onion, thinly sliced
- 1 tbsp fresh dill

Instructions:

1. Spoon cottage cheese into a bowl.
2. Top with smoked salmon, capers, red onion, and fresh dill.

Cheesy Grits with Butter & Poached Egg

Ingredients:

- 1 cup stone-ground grits
- 4 cups water or milk
- 1/2 cup shredded cheddar cheese
- 1 tbsp butter
- 2 poached eggs
- Salt & black pepper

Instructions:

1. Cook grits in water/milk over low heat until thick.
2. Stir in butter, cheese, salt, and pepper.
3. Top with poached eggs before serving.

Avocado & Turkey Breakfast Wrap

Ingredients:

- 1 whole wheat tortilla
- 2 slices turkey breast
- 1/2 avocado, mashed
- 1 scrambled egg
- 1 tbsp Greek yogurt
- 1/4 tsp black pepper

Instructions:

1. Spread mashed avocado on the tortilla.
2. Layer with turkey, scrambled egg, and Greek yogurt.
3. Season with black pepper and roll up.

Roasted Veggie & Egg Breakfast Bowl

Ingredients:

- 1/2 cup roasted sweet potatoes
- 1/2 cup roasted bell peppers
- 1/2 cup sautéed kale
- 2 fried eggs
- 1 tbsp feta cheese
- 1/2 tsp smoked paprika

Instructions:

1. Roast sweet potatoes and bell peppers at **400°F (200°C) for 20 minutes**.
2. Sauté kale until wilted.
3. Assemble in a bowl and top with fried eggs, feta, and smoked paprika.

Greek Yogurt & Savory Granola Bowl

Ingredients:

- 1 cup Greek yogurt
- 1/2 cup savory granola (oats, nuts, seeds, rosemary, and olive oil)
- 1 tbsp honey
- 1 tbsp pumpkin seeds

Instructions:

1. Spoon Greek yogurt into a bowl.
2. Top with savory granola, pumpkin seeds, and a drizzle of honey.

Breakfast Polenta with Garlic & Herbs

Ingredients:

- 1 cup polenta
- 4 cups water or broth
- 1 tbsp butter
- 1 tsp garlic powder
- 1 tbsp fresh herbs (parsley, basil, thyme)
- Salt & black pepper

Instructions:

1. Cook polenta in water/broth, stirring until thick.
2. Stir in butter, garlic powder, and herbs.
3. Season with salt and black pepper before serving.

Scrambled Eggs with Chorizo & Peppers

Ingredients:

- 3 eggs
- 1/2 cup cooked chorizo
- 1/4 cup diced bell peppers
- 1 tbsp butter
- Salt & black pepper

Instructions:

1. Sauté bell peppers and chorizo in butter until soft.
2. Whisk eggs and pour into the pan.
3. Stir constantly until cooked through.

Croque Madame with Gruyère & Ham

Ingredients:

- 2 slices brioche or sourdough bread
- 2 slices ham
- 1/2 cup grated Gruyère cheese
- 1 tbsp Dijon mustard
- 1 tbsp butter
- 1 egg, fried

Instructions:

1. Assemble sandwich with ham, cheese, and Dijon mustard.
2. Butter and toast in a skillet until golden.
3. Top with a fried egg before serving.

www.ingramcontent.com/pod-product-compliance
Lightning Source LLC
LaVergne TN
LVHW081505060526
838201LV00056BA/2936